# AMAZING HISTORY

# PIRATES

## NEIL MORRIS

A+

**Smart Apple Media**

Published by Smart Apple Media
2140 Howard Drive West
North Mankato, MN 56003

Created by Q2A Media
Series Editor: Jean Coppendale
Designers: Diksha Khatri, Ashita Murgai
Picture Researchers: Lalit Dalal, Jyoti Sachdev
Illustrators: Hemant Arya, Adil A Siddiqui, Amir Khan, Manish Prasad, Prashant Jogi, Subhash Vohra

Picture Credits:
t=top b=bottom l=left r=right m=middle
Cover images: Bettmann/ Corbis: background, Sherwin McGehee/ Istockphoto: b,
Back cover: Q2A Media: tl, Linda Bucklin/ Shutterstock: tm, Pepbaix | Dreamstime.com: tr
Q2A Media: 4t, 6t, 6b, 9b, 12bl, 13, 14, 17, 18mr, 19, 20, 26t, 27b, 3LH-Fine Art/ Superstock: 4b, Corbis: 5t,
The British Library Board: 7t, Baldwin H. Ward & Kathryn C. Ward/ Corbis: 8b, The Bridgeman Art Library/ Photolibrary: 12br,
Albert Cheng/ Shutterstock: 15, T.W./ Shutterstock: 16, DGID/ Istockphoto: 18bl, Aris Vidalis/ Istockphoto: 18br,
Library of Congress: 21t, 22b, 26b, 27t, Bettmann/ Corbis: 21b, National Maritime Museum, London: 23t, Scott Rothstein/
Shutterstock: 24t, Jubal Harshaw/ Shutterstock: 24b.

Printed in China

Library of Congress Cataloging-in-Publication Data

Morris, Neil, 1946–
Pirates / by Neil Morris.
p. cm. — (Amazing history)
ISBN 978-1-59920-104-7
1. Pirates-Juvenile literature. I. Title.

G535.M67 2007
910.4'5–dc22      2007014722

First Edition

9 8 7 6 5 4 3 2 1

# Contents

# What is a pirate?

The word pirate means "robber at sea." For as long as ships have crossed the oceans, taking goods from one port to another, there have been pirates eager to rob them.

## Thieves at sea

Stories and movies often show pirates as exciting adventurers, but most of them were just blood-thirsty thieves! Many pirates chose their way of life because they thought it was a way to get rich quickly, and some men were criminals escaping the law. Others were kidnapped and forced into a life of piracy.

**Pirate flag**
The skull-and-crossbones, also called the **Jolly Roger**

**Fierce attack**
Pirate leaders were brutal, desperate men

Pirates attacked ships for gold, jewels, sugar, spices, tobacco, medicine, and rum.

Chinese pirates sailed Asian seas in armed **junks**. They sometimes attacked European ships in groups.

**Bamboo**
Strengthened the junk's sails

# Pirate hunting grounds

When Spain controlled the South American colonies in the 1500s, Spanish treasure fleets came under attack. Barbary pirates, or **corsairs**, had bases in Algiers and attacked ships from Spain, France, and Italy. In the early 1600s, Asian pirates attacked European ships. Fleets of Chinese pirates terrorized the coast in the 1800s. When ships of the East India Company traded between Europe and Asia in the seventeenth and eighteenth centuries, the Indian Ocean became the pirates' hunting ground.

## HOT SPOTS

*The famous pirate Captain William Kidd was hired as a **privateer**, but he turned to piracy and made a fortune robbing ships in the Indian Ocean.*

# Barbary corsairs

During the 1500s, bands of sea robbers, called corsairs, worked along the **Barbary Coast** in North Africa. They **looted** ships and sold crews into slavery.

## Ruthless red beards

Arouj and Khair-ed-Din were the most feared Barbary corsairs. They had red beards and were called the "Barbarossa" brothers. Both led big corsair fleets. Arouj was killed in 1518 by the Spaniards, but his brother continued to fight against their Christian enemies.

Khair-ed-Din, one of the fierce Barbarossa brothers.

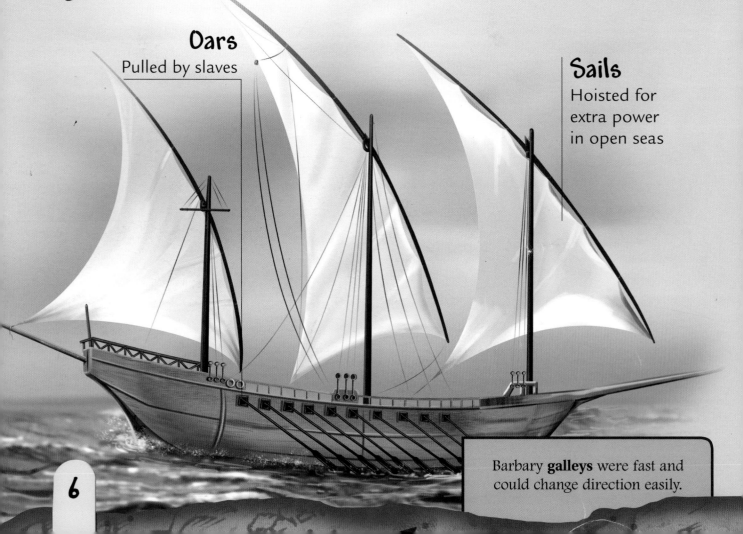

**Oars**
Pulled by slaves

**Sails**
Hoisted for extra power in open seas

Barbary **galleys** were fast and could change direction easily.

Pages from a book called *The History of the Barbary Corsairs*, written in 1637. The pictures show the various methods of torture the corsairs used on their captives.

# Turning Turk

Most of the Barbary Coast was under **Muslim** rule. The corsairs were after treasure from the ships as well as Christians to sell into slavery. In the 1600s, many Europeans joined the Muslims. Dutch pirate Simon Danziger and privateer Jan Jansz joined up with the Barbary corsairs. Jansz raided Iceland and captured and **enslaved** at least 400 islanders. In 1607, English **nobleman** Sir Francis Verney "turned Turk" and joined the Barbary corsairs. One of his prizes included an English trading ship that was carrying French wine for the king's table.

## HOT SPOTS

*The name "Barbary" comes from the Latin and Greek and means "foreign" or "strange." It is related to the word "barbarian," which the Romans used for all foreigners who lived on the outskirts of their empire.*

# Privateers

Queen Elizabeth I of England hated Catholic Spain, and she wanted Spanish treasure. The queen was happy when her sea captains raided Spanish ships that were bringing back gold and silver from captured lands in South America.

## Pirating hero

Elizabeth's favorite "pirate" was Francis Drake. For 30 years, he led one attack after another on the Spanish fleet, **plundering** enemy ships and collecting a fortune. In his ship the *Golden Hind,* Drake regularly attacked Spanish treasure **galleons**. He presented Elizabeth with jewels, 13 chests of golden dishes, and tons of silver and gold.

Elizabeth I thanked and honored Drake by knighting him on board the *Golden Hind* in 1581.

### HOT SPOTS

*Queen Elizabeth I was so pleased with her "sea dogs," or pirate captains, that she made them all knights. As well as Sir Francis Drake, there were Sir Martin Frobisher, Sir Humphrey Gilbert, Sir Richard Grenville, and Sir Richard Hawkins.*

# License to steal

Governments gave out **licenses**, called "**letters of marque**," that allowed sailors to attack and rob enemy ships. Seamen who had the letter could not be accused of piracy, which was punishable by death. Instead, those working for the government were called privateers. Unlike pirates, privateers had to share their stolen **booty** with their king or queen.

## Mainmast
The largest mast with the biggest sails

The *Golden Hind*, in which Sir Francis Drake sailed around the world. The ship was 120 feet (36.5 m) long.

## Crow's nest
Where a guard could stand

# Caribbean buccaneers

Around the early 1600s, outlaws from Europe escaped to the Caribbean islands. These offered an excellent hideout. The first **buccaneers** were French adventurers who lived on **Hispaniola**.

## Meat smokers

The buccaneers took their name from the French word *boucan*, a grill for smoking meat. They lived a fierce life, hunting wild boar and selling dried meat to passing ships for gunpowder and supplies. When they discovered that hunting ships brought bigger prizes, they decided to become pirates. More and more convicts and escaped slaves soon joined them.

### Treasure galleon
Slow and difficult to sail when fully loaded

### Boarding vessel
Out of the galleon's firing line

A pirate boarding party approaching a treasure ship in the Caribbean. Pirate ships were usually smaller, faster, and able to catch their prey quickly, once they had spotted it.

Henry Morgan attacked towns in Central and South America. He forced his victims to give up their treasure—or face torture or death.

# Henry Morgan

Welshman Henry Morgan (1635–88) gathered a pirate army and led raids on Spanish ships and colonies. Licensed to rob, he destroyed Panama City, the largest Spanish city in Central America, in 1671. He attacked with 38 ships and 2,000 men. This pleased the British, and King Charles II made him a knight and deputy governor of Jamaica. Sir Henry collected a fortune as a royal pirate, but drank himself to death.

## HOT SPOTS

*Frenchman François L'Olonnais (1630–68) was a particularly cruel buccaneer. He was known to hack his victims to death with his **cutlass** and then lick the blood from the blade.*

# Beware, pirates!

Pirates closely watched the ports to find out which ships had the richest cargoes. They knew the routes treasure ships took and waited for their prey in shallow waters. Pirates preferred to capture their enemies without a fight.

## Surprise attack

Pirates often followed their victims for days, keeping just out of sight. Then, they would suddenly appear, fire their cannons, and shout and make a lot of noise. Pirates tried not to damage the ship in case they could use it for themselves, especially if their own ship was damaged.

Grappling hook

In the Bay of Bengal in 1800, French privateer Robert Surcouf used his small, fast ship to attack and capture *The Kent*, a much bigger British ship.

# Taking the ship

When they were at close range, pirates aimed cannonballs at the enemy ship. Then, they sailed alongside the ship and threw grappling hooks into the **rigging**. The sharp hooks caught in the ropes. The pirates pulled the ships together and jumped aboard, screaming and shouting. There was fierce fighting, but the pirates usually outnumbered the crew and took their prize.

The three stages of a pirate ship's attack were fast and furious.

## HOT SPOTS

*Pirates sometimes tricked their victims by flying a friendly flag as they sailed toward them. Then, when it was too late to escape, the pirates would run up their black flag, and if there was no surrender, they would attack!*

First, the pirates fired at the victim.

Then, they pulled in close . . .

. . . and leaped aboard, armed to the teeth.

# Pirate weapons

Pirates used a wide range of weapons to capture the ships they boarded. But first, they had to get on board.

## Cannonballs

Pirates fired iron cannonballs to stop and damage enemy ships. A cannonball that struck the opponent's **hull** could cause a lot of injuries to the crew from flying splinters of wood. Another tactic was to use chain-shot. This involved chaining two cannonballs together and firing them at enemy masts and sails to bring them down.

**One . . .**
Ram gunpowder into the barrel

**Two . . .**
Roll in a cannonball

The gunner loaded a cannon and then fired it from a gun port on the main deck.

**Three . . . Fire!**
Light the fuse

# Flintlock and cutlass

**Flintlock pistols** were the pirates' favorite boarding weapons. They had a short barrel and were easy to carry. But reloading was slow, so most pirates did not bother and just clubbed the enemy with the hard end. In hand-to-hand fights, pirates also used the cut-throat cutlass to slash at their opponents and daggers to stab them.

When the trigger of a flintlock pistol was pulled, the flint inside struck a metal plate. This created sparks that lit the gunpowder and fired the shot. The longer **musket** was fired from the shoulder.

## Cutlass
A short, broad blade with a hand guard

## Musket
Used before boarding to kill the man steering the enemy ship

## Flintlock pistol
Light and easy to carry

## HOT SPOTS

*At close range, pirates often threw stinkpots on the deck of the enemy ship. These were small, clay pots that were usually filled with a burning mixture of tar and rags. These caused clouds of foul-smelling smoke, which created panic and made eyes water.*

15

# Pirate ships

What makes a good pirate ship? The answer is . . . SPEED! Most pirates did not build their own ships. Instead, they stole ones that they captured. Then, they added extra guns or changed the rigging to make them faster.

**Topsail**
Provided added speed when necessary

## Speedy sloops

From the early 1700s, pirates went after speedy **sloops** and larger **schooners** with big sails. Up to 75 pirates could squeeze on board, and the ships carried 14 guns. They were perfect for the hit-and-run techniques of the pirate trade. Single-masted sloops were favorites with Caribbean pirates.

Schooners were sleek, fast, and very popular with American privateers. Most had two masts, but some had up to four.

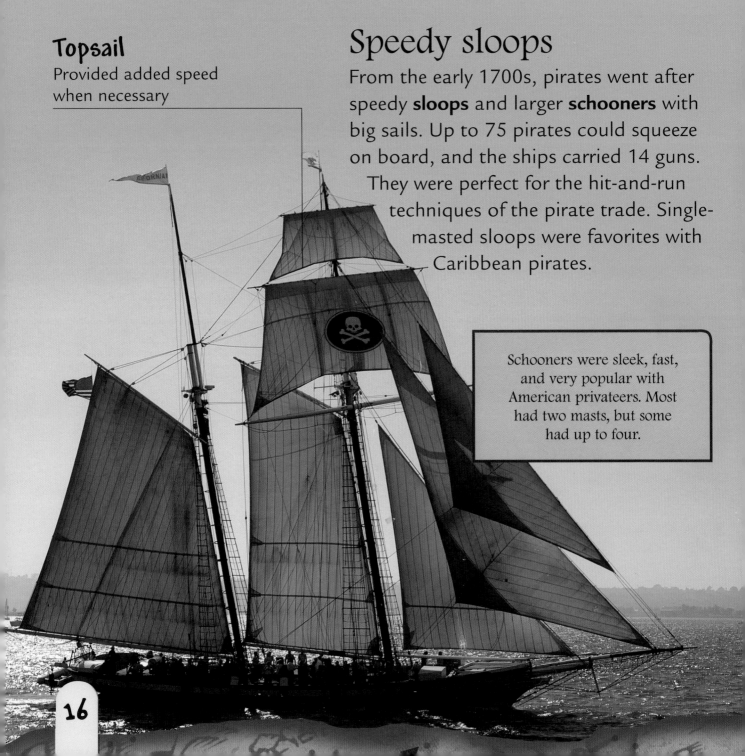

**Mizzen**
Extra mast at the **stern**

**Long oars**
Called sweeps

Captain Kidd's ship, the *Adventure Galley*, could be rowed when there was no wind.

# Adventure galley

The *Adventure Galley* was built in 1695 for William Kidd, the famous Scottish-born privateer, to hunt pirates—before he became one himself. The ship was 125 feet (38 m) long and could reach a speed of 14 knots, or 16 miles (26 km) per hour. It had 34 guns that fired 12-pound (5.4 kg) cannonballs ("twelve-pounders"), and Kidd's crew had 1,000 spare cannonballs for refills. Unfortunately, this brilliant ship had problems with leaks!

## HOTSPOTS

*Chinese pirates captured cargo ships and stocked them with guns and cannons. Big fighting junks were about 100 feet (30 m) long and could carry up to 400 men. The junk's sails were made of bamboo matting.*

# Life on the high seas

Life on board a pirate ship was tough and dangerous. At night, the crew slept in the small, smelly hold. Water slopped below, and there were rats everywhere.

## Hardtack

Long-lasting crackers made from flour and water were the pirates' basic food. These crackers, called hardtack, were stale and usually full of wriggling weevils. It was best to eat them in the dark and wash them down with gulps of beer. Sometimes they ate dried, salted meat, but it was hard to chew. Some crews kept chickens for their eggs, which they called "cackle fruit."

**Beer**
Kept better than
fresh water

**Turtle meat**
A pirate delicacy

**Crackers**
Hard and tough

# Sour medicine

Fresh fruit and vegetables did not keep on long sea journeys, and many pirates became sick with **scurvy** from a lack of vitamin C. In 1753, it was discovered that eating limes could prevent the disease. Conditions on board were filthy, and sickness and infection spread easily. Injured limbs were just sawn off—usually by the ship's carpenter and without any painkillers.

## HOT SPOTS

*Although pirates led a lawless life, most crews had rules and regulations. Pirate captain Bartholomew Roberts had a strict code of conduct for the men on his ship. He banned all swearing, drinking, and gambling on board.*

Medical supplies were precious and rare.

## Surgery
Patient had to be held down

It was best to avoid injury. Surgery was extremely painful.

# Blackbeard

Edward Teach was known as Blackbeard. He terrorized the North American coast and was one of the fiercest men in the history of piracy. In 1717, he **blockaded** Charleston, South Carolina, plundered ships, and kidnapped rich citizens.

## Huge terror

Blackbeard was a huge man. He twisted the ends of his beard into braids and tied them with ribbons looped over his ears. He carried several pistols and sometimes fired them under the table while eating with his crew. Blackbeard once filled the hold of his ship with sulfur fumes to see how long his crew could stay there. He was so cruel that he drove his own men to mutiny.

NORTH AMERICA

South Carolina

**Charleston**

### Burning hair
Blackbeard braided pieces of cord into his hair, which were set on fire to look more frightening in battle

### Swords
Two swords and several knives with very sharp blades

### Pistols
Three pairs of pistols

When Blackbeard went into battle, he terrified the enemy. He was known for being ruthless and cruel.

# Blackbeard's last stand

In 1718, Lieutenant Robert Maynard chased the fearsome pirate with two sloops and 60 men. Blackbeard escaped when the sloops **ran aground**, calling Maynard's men "cowardly puppies." With the rising tide, Maynard's sloop broke free and caught up with the pirate ship. In a brutal hand-to-hand fight and after receiving five pistol shots and 20 sword wounds, Blackbeard was killed. Maynard cut off his head and threw his body overboard. Legend says that his body swam around the ship twice before sinking.

## HOT SPOTS

*Blackbeard's ship, Queen Anne's Revenge, was the largest pirate ship ever. The wreck was found in 1996 by divers off the coast of North Carolina.*

Blackbeard put up a tremendous fight with a sword and pistol before he was finally killed.

Blackbeard's head was hung on Maynard's ship for all to see.

# Women pirates

Women were not welcome on board pirate ships. But they fought just as bravely and were just as ruthless as male pirates. Adventurous women, such as Anne Bonney and Mary Read, dressed up as men and became pirates.

## Bonney and Calico Jack

Anne Bonney fell in love with pirate captain Jack Rackham, called Calico Jack because of his coarse cloth pants. She dressed up as a man and joined Jack's crew. Rackham was hanged in 1720. Anne Bonney was released because she was pregnant. When Calico Jack was at the gallows, she told him, "Had you fought like a man, you need not have hanged like a dog!"

This was the flag of pirate captain Jack Rackham, which showed crossed cutlasses instead of bones.

Mary Read (right) made friends with Anne Bonney (left) when Calico Jack captured her ship. From 1718, the pair raided Spanish treasure ships.

The Chinese pirate leader Madame Cheng was a fierce warrior. Armed with a cutlass, she feared no man.

# Madame Cheng

In the early nineteenth century, the South China Sea was controlled by Ching Shih, who became known as Madame Cheng. She was the widow of Cheng I, who controlled a vast fleet of pirate junks. Between 1807 and 1810, more than 70,000 pirates looted under Madame Cheng's ruthless command—she punished any theft by beheading. In 1810, she bought a pardon from the Chinese government.

## HOT SPOTS

*About 1,500 years ago, Goth princess Alvilda from Sweden sailed off with an all-woman crew to avoid marrying a Danish prince. They became pirates and preyed on ships along the coast of Denmark.*

# Treasure trove

Pirates were always on the lookout for valuable goods that were easy to sell. Their favorite treasures were gold, silver, and precious jewels. They found all these on ships sailing back to Europe from the Americas.

Many pirate maps have been found over the years but few of them are real.

### X marks the spot
Where the treasure was buried

### Doubloon
The most valuable Spanish gold coin

### Cross
Used as a guide to break the coin into halves or quarters

## Buried treasure

Pirates generally looked for a quick sale for their booty, but sometimes, they had to hide it. There have been many tales of hidden **hoards**, but these were mostly myths. However, Captain Kidd really did bury his treasure, but not on a desert island. In 1699, he hid his loot on Gardiners Island, just off the coast of New York. Most of it was found, but some has never been discovered.

Coins from Spain and other countries were popular with pirates for their precious metals and also for what they could buy.

## Captain Kidd
Keeps a sharp eye on the burial of his treasure

## Crew
Digs a deep hole to bury the booty

## Treasure chest
Marked WK for William Kidd

# Sharing the spoils

A hold full of gold was every pirate's dream. The captain and his officers usually received a special share of the loot, but otherwise, it was split evenly among the crew. Usually, two shares were given to the captain, one and a half shares to the ship's master and doctor, one and one-fourth shares to the first mate, gunner, and **boatswain**, and one share to ordinary crew members. The loot might be worth millions of dollars at today's values.

## HOT SPOTS

*In 1671, Welsh pirate Henry Morgan raided Panama City, but his buccaneers found little loot to share. In 1927, hoards of gold and silver were found in the Church of San José in Panama. The treasure may have been hidden in the church before Morgan's attack.*

# Pirate punishment

Pirates always hoped that their crimes would pay. But very few lived to enjoy their wealth, and throughout history, captured pirates faced a horrible death. In Roman times, they were crucified, and in later centuries, they were beheaded or hanged.

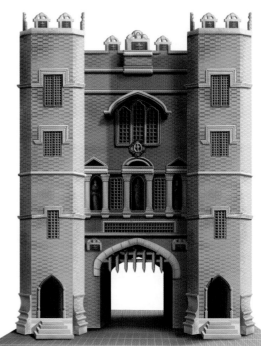

Newgate Prison in London was a fearsome place. Kidd was held there for a year.

Captain Kidd's corpse was hung from a wooden frame called a gibbet.

## Horrible warning

In England, pirates were tried and then usually executed. In 1701, William Kidd had to go through his hanging twice, after the first rope snapped. His corpse was chained to a post over the Thames River to be washed over by the tide three times. It was then covered in tar and put in an iron cage to serve as a horrible warning to would-be pirates.

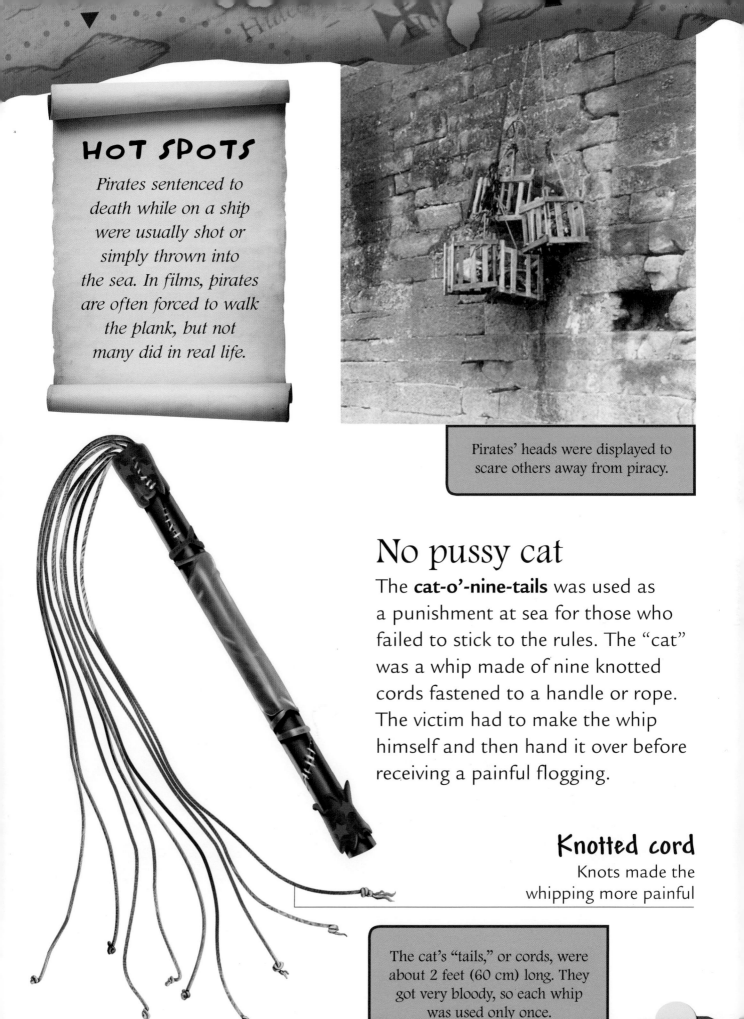

Pirates sentenced to death while on a ship were usually shot or simply thrown into the sea. In films, pirates are often forced to walk the plank, but not many did in real life.

Pirates' heads were displayed to scare others away from piracy.

## No pussy cat

The **cat-o'-nine-tails** was used as a punishment at sea for those who failed to stick to the rules. The "cat" was a whip made of nine knotted cords fastened to a handle or rope. The victim had to make the whip himself and then hand it over before receiving a painful flogging.

### Knotted cord

Knots made the whipping more painful

The cat's "tails," or cords, were about 2 feet (60 cm) long. They got very bloody, so each whip was used only once.

27

# Pirates today

Piracy continues today in the South China Sea, Indonesia, Bangladesh, Vietnam, India, Nigeria, and the ports and rivers of Brazil. Pirates hide in inlets and on islands.

## Speed and surprise

Modern pirates favor fast, small boats and attack where large boats and yachts have to slow down to **navigate** through narrow straits. Pirate boats are often disguised as fishing boats or cargo boats that are manned by heavily armed, violent gangs. They steal the cargo and any valuables on board. Sometimes, they take over the entire ship and demand a **ransom** for the safe return of the crew.

### Hood
Worn so that thieves cannot be recognized

Today's pirates still rely on surprise. To the victims, they seem to rush in from nowhere.

# High-tech piracy

Modern pirates often use high-tech equipment to attack and steal from merchant ships and **cruise ships**. They may track the route of the ship using inside information supplied by someone who works for the shipping company. They may also hack into ships' computers and listen to telephone calls. They can use radar and cell phones to follow their victims and then make their deadly, surprise attacks.

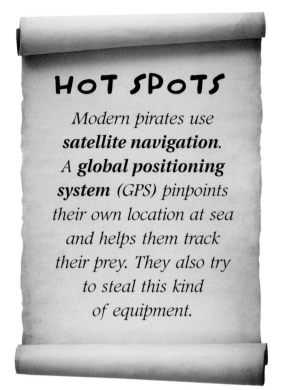

## HOT SPOTS

*Modern pirates use **satellite navigation**. A **global positioning system** (GPS) pinpoints their own location at sea and helps them track their prey. They also try to steal this kind of equipment.*

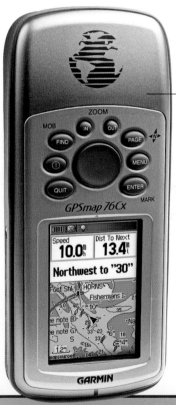

## Waterproof
Specially made for use at sea

This hand-held GPS device is only 6 inches (15 cm) long.

Modern-day pirates and smugglers also use radar to keep track of a ship's progress and follow its route, in case they want to attack.

## Radar warning
A sailor checks his radar screen to see if there are any ships nearby.

# Glossary

**Barbary Coast** The Mediterranean coast of North Africa.

**blockaded** Prevented people from entering or leaving a place.

**boatswain** (Pronounced bo-sun) A ship's officer, in charge of equipment.

**booty** Valuable stolen goods.

**buccaneers** Pirates or privateers who raided Spanish ships and colonies in the West Indies.

**cat-o'-nine-tails** A whip used for flogging.

**corsairs** Pirates or privateers of the Mediterranean region.

**cruise ships** Large passenger ships that take vacationers on a trip.

**cutlass** A short sword with a curved blade.

**enslaved** Made someone a slave.

**flintlock pistols** Early guns in which a flint spark lit gunpowder.

**galleons** Large, three-masted sailing ships, used especially by the Spanish.

**galleys** Large ships powered by oars and, sometimes, sails.

**global positioning system** (GPS) A network of transmitters and satellites that can pinpoint a ship's location.

**Hispaniola** A large Caribbean island, making up the countries of present-day Haiti and the Dominican Republic.

**hoards** Hidden stores of valuable goods.

**hull** The main body of a ship.

**Jolly Roger** A pirate flag.

**junks** Chinese sailing ships.

**letters of marque** An official license, giving authority to attack enemy ships.

**licenses** Official, written permissions.

**looted** Stole goods.

**musket** An early gun with a long barrel.

**Muslim** A follower of the religion of Islam.

**navigate** To follow a course and find the right way.

**nobleman** A man who belongs to a high social class.

**plundering** Stealing goods.

**privateer** Someone who is legally authorized to attack enemy ships.

**ransom** Money paid for the release of a prisoner.

**rigging** Ropes that support a ship's masts and control the sails.

**ran aground** Hit the seabed in shallow water.

**satellite navigation** A method of finding your way by information from satellites.

**schooners** Small, fast, two- or three-masted sailing ships.

**scurvy** A disease caused by a lack of vitamin C. Sailors caught it by not eating enough fresh fruit and vegetables. Scurvy caused bleeding gums and sores on the skin.

**sloops** Small, light, single-masted sailing ships.

**stern** The rear part of a ship.

# Index

# Web sites

www.thepiratesrealm.com    A source for information about famous pirates, ships, and flags.

www.nationalgeographic.com/pirates    National Geographic presents a High Seas Adventure.

www.nmm.ac.uk/server/show/conWebDoc.159    Information from the National Maritime Museum of the United Kingdom, with a link to a Time Pirates game.

www.thewayofthepirates.com    Includes life stories of Blackbeard, Calico Jack, and Sir Francis Drake.

disney.go.com/disneypictures/pirates    Web site of the Disney movie *Pirates of the Caribbean*.